Opiate Addiction

A Step by Step Guide to Overcoming Opiate Addiction Forever

Rock Bankole

Digital Print House

BE A BETTER YOU

Table of Contents

INTRODUCTION

Humans have been using opiate drugs since thousands of years and still continue to use them despite knowing the damages they cause to one's health.

Opiates are drugs, most commonly used for inducing sleep and relieving pain, they are also known as narcotics and opioids. These drugs are made from opium which is obtained from the poppy plant. Opiates can be in a tar-like substance form or brownish or white powder. Most common types of opioids are methadone, hydrocodone, heroin, codeine, oxycodone (OxyContin), Dilaudid, fentanyl, and morphine.

Opiates tend to increase the quantity of dopamine which is released in the reward system of the brain and it then mimics the effects of "endogenous opioids". When Heroin is injected in any vein, it reaches the brain in about 15 to 20 seconds and then binds to the receptors of opiate which are found in many different regions of brain, like the reward system. When the receptors activate in the reward circuits they cause a very brief rush of intense euphoria, which is then followed by a few hours of contented and relaxed state.

Opiates are a medical necessity as they help in relieving pain. These are legal by prescription, except for heroin. People who use them for relieving their pain, 1% of them become addicted. Also, people tend to develop problems who use opiates to "get high"; this gives feelings of peace and intense pleasure.

Some of the people who experiment with opioids might start with its oral use, sniffing, snorting etc., but they often then progress to intravenous (IV) utilization as it is stronger. When the damage has affected the veins due to IV utilization and it cannot be used anymore, then the logical substitutes are the hypodermic injections. This is known as "muscling" or "skin popping" among its many other terms.

Skin popping or IV usually lead to life-threatening heart infections, abscesses, HIV/AIDS or Hepatitis B or C, as most of the drugs found on streets are not clean.

Addiction! What is it? This is a person's' relationship with drugs. The amount of drug utilization is more than a person's recommended use and despite its negative consequences, they continue using them.

Drugs are used for relaxing or escaping but over the time the body gets used to the drugs and you find it difficult to live without them and find pleasure using them. It damages an individual's self-esteem to a great extent.

Roughly, about 10% of the entire population is addicted to alcohol or drugs. Victims who get addicted to these drugs make sure they are getting their next dose on time. Addiction can also cause people to take an overdose which can be life threatening. Excess of everything is harmful! Whether opiate is injected, snorted or smoked, it has harmful and serious effects.

CHAPTER 1 - COMMON OPIATES AND THEIR UTILIZATION

Opiates are drugs made from the opium poppy to relief pain. An opioid is the term which is used when referring to the "entire class of drugs" which also includes synthetic opiates like OxyContin. Opioids were basically developed in order to get drugs which could act longer. They are usually produced in forms which can easily be injected or taken by mouth.

Opiates can be gained naturally or they can be man-made. Opiates occurring naturally include opium, morphine, and codeine.

OPIATES AND WITH THEIR GENERIC NAMES:

- Heroin
- Oxycodone (Percocet, OxyContin)
- Methadone
- Morphine (MS Contin Kadian)
- Hydrocodone (Vicodin, Hycodan)
- Codeine
- Hydromorphone (Dilaudid)
- Duragesic (fentanyl)

Heroin is produced from morphine which comes from the opium poppy. Heroin is basically a street drug in most of the countries, and it is never found in its pure form. It is mixed with various other substances and is normally contaminated. The needles which are used to inject it are often contaminated as well.

OxyContin is the longer acting variant of oxycodone which is meant to be taken by mouth. It is a useful drug for people who suffer from chronic pain like cancer, but it can be harmful if abused. If it is crushed and bitten or swallowed, it does not act long and absorbs rapidly. Some people also crush it, then dissolve it in saline and later inject it into their bodies. This is more likely to lead to an overdose and can be fatal.

Codeine is also used in treating pain, but it is usually combined with other medications. It is found in opium poppy in very small amounts.

Hydrocodone and Oxycodone (Percodan and Percocet) are the short-acting anodyne (pain killers) which are mixed with aspirin or acetaminophen. It is less likely that they are abused, but exceptions are always there.

Methadone is also amongst long-acting opioid which is used widely for treating heroin addiction. If given once every day, it is unlikely to produce a "high" feeling, but it prevents withdrawal symptoms. Like OxyContin, it is also medically used for chronic pain.

Morphine comes in from the opium poppy and is widely known as a pain reliever. It could be injected or taken by mouth but can also be abused. It is one of the shortest acting drugs, but its long-acting type is also present known as MS Contin which should specifically be taken by mouth. But if it is injected or crushed and swallowed, then it is not a long acting drug anymore and can result in fatal overdose.

CHAPTER 2 - OPIATE ADDICTION

Euphoria or the sense of wellbeing produced by opiates can be addictive for some people. Legitimately, opiates are utilized for treating pain. When consuming opiates in order to alleviate pain, many people tend to grow tolerance. This means that people need more in order to get the same effect. A few of them then get addicted to opiates. They start to think obsessively about taking more opiates and in some cases, they also engage themselves in illegal activities including double doctoring.

If a high dose of opiates is taken, it can cause a person to die from a respiratory or cardiac arrest. Tolerance of a person to the opiates' euphoric effect grows faster as compared to the tolerance to its dangerous effects. Consequently, people frequently take an overdose mistakenly just because they try to get a little more "high" and take in too much.

Overdoses are very common and are a threat to life. They take place because the people addicted to drugs are unaware of the strength they have bought or it is because people have grown tolerance and they need a better "high" feeling.

If the addicted person is very sleepy and has compressed pupils, they require serious medical attention in order to prevent death from overdosing.

An overdose of opiates can be reversed in the hospital by naltrexone given intravenously. Always contact an emergency service if there is any feeling of danger of an overdose.

CRITERIA FOR ADDICTION

An addicted person should be able to meet at the least 3 of the criteria's given below.

(The following is based on the criterion of World Health Organization and the American Psychiatric Association).

- **Tolerance**. Has your opiates utilization increased over time?
- **Withdrawal**. When you stop using, do you experience symptoms of withdrawal such as irritability, nausea, anxiety, vomiting, sweats or shakes? Emotional withdrawal is equally important as the physical withdrawal.
- **Limited control**. Is your utilization more than the dose prescribed or more than you like to? Do you regret after taking opiates?
- **Negative consequences**. Have you ever experienced negative results after using opiates to mood, health, family, job or self-esteem?
- **Postponed or neglected activities**. Have you been unable to do certain activities because of the drug use like work, household, recreational or social activities?
- **Significant energy or time spent**. Do you obsessively think about getting and/or using drugs? Have you ever minimized or concealed your use of opiates? Have you ever thought of avoiding opiates?

- **The desire to curtail the use**. Have you ever thought of controlling or cutting down opiate use? Have you been unsuccessful at cutting down your use of opiates?

HOW DOES OPIATE ADDICTION FEEL?

Addictive substances make a person feel good and relaxed because they energize the brain's pleasure center through the neurotransmitters like GABA and dopamine. If you have a genetic sensitivity, the addictive substances make you feel so good that you never want to give up on them.

This is actually where the addiction comes in. Due to genetic sensitivity (predisposition), you are also willing to bear the negative consequences to getting more and to keep feeling the high.

Denial is the biggest part of addiction. Because addictive substances like opiates feel good, the addict will at the beginning deny that they have a problem. Long-term consequences involve isolation from activities and people, and this is when they know they are addicted to opiates.

EFFECTS OF OPIATE ADDICTION

The most important effects of opiate addiction involve psychological, social and emotional. People commonly think of the economic and physical consequences of addiction.

Psychological or Mental Effects – Abuse of opiates declines the mental health. Negative mental and psychological effects of using opiates includes:

- Extreme changes in behavior or mood swings
- Disillusioned, misrepresented percept of reality
- Relying on opiates for contentment and feelings of happiness
- Frequent experience of anxiety and depression
- Mental clouding
- Reduced sex drive

Physical Effects –abuse of opiates could disable normal functioning of the body as systems and organs are slowly destroyed. Physical effects include:

- Cardiovascular complications
- Difficulties in digesting, like constipation, bleeding, vomiting and stomach cramping
- Hyperalgesia – heightened perception of pain
- Dehydration of mucous and skin membranes
- Jaundice
- Decreased immunity
- Swelling
- Pulmonary issues
- Vision problems
- Death due to toxicity or overdose

Social Effects –opiates abuse can cause various negative social effects. These include:

- Disaffection from social functions
- Division within the family unit
- Isolation or withdrawal from family and friends
- Poor relationships with loved ones
- Decreased participation or lack of interest in activities

Addiction damages your self-esteem and your relationships. These damages are deep and take long to repair. You've hurt family and friends. You have frustrated yourself. In life, you have traded many important things so you can make more time for opiates utilization. You have seen the pain in the eyes of your family. These are those consequences which can motivate you towards recovery.

OPIATE TREATMENT AND HELP

Never let opiate addiction take control of your life. In reality, everyone is able to make decisions about seeking help to overcome opiate addiction with a treatment center or a rehab so they can live a free and peaceful life. The very first step that can lead towards overcoming the addiction is to recognize that you require help and ask for it.

Getting professional help is important to appropriately deal with complications that might have resulted from the use of opiates. Suffering from an opiate addiction can be an isolating and an overpowering experience, but it is essential to remember that you are not alone. Taking help from an opiate professional team can give you the best treatment and care.

CHAPTER 3-OVERCOMING OPIATE ADDICTION

Opioid addiction is not a mental or moral weakness. It is a chronic/continuing medical condition which results from changes that take place in the brains of susceptible people. Once the addiction of narcotics is developed, escaping this cycle can be a long-term process.

Addictions of opiates can damage the body as well as the brain. When the damage is caused to the body, it needs some time to heal. During this healing and repairing time, a person is likely to experience uncomfortable withdrawal effects and these can easily drive them back again to opiate utilization.

No one can overcome addictions in a few days, it takes time. Give time to yourself and your body to adjust to the changes. If opiates dosage is suddenly discontinued withdrawal will occur.

With some planning and a great amount of determination, anyone can overcome their addiction of opiate. Never lose hope and follow proper steps.

STEP 1: MAKING A RECOVERY PLAN

- Never feel shameful or guilty.
- Recover with people who are also going through the same condition. This makes the recovering process easier.
- Be honest to yourself and practice to share your feelings.
- Avoid situation which involve a higher risk.

- Learn strategies that might prevent you from relapsing.

Step 2: Factors to consider before choosing the type of treatment

If you or your loved one is an opiate addict and is ready to seek professional help, then there are many different factors to consider before choosing the treatment. It's very important that you opt for a treatment which will be effective and will provide the greatest level of care during your recovery process. Following are the factors that you might consider when opting for an opiate addiction treatment:

- Cost of treatment and whether an insurance is included or not
- Location of the treatment center etc. Some individuals might prefer seeking help from somewhere close to their home and some might prefer going far away for their treatment.
- Choose the type of treatment; whether inpatient or outpatient (discussed later in this book)
- How successful has the treatment been for the previous opiate addicts? Always get information about the success rate of the treatment center.

At last, the best treatment for you would be the one that allow for an individualized care and treatment which is according to your individual needs. The treatment centers first assess your current position, health, and addiction level and then prepare a treatment plan for you. From this, the treatment plan that has been prepared will keep changing based on different elements of your recovery as you go on.

The best time for seeking help is now! Opiate addiction treatment could assist you in getting your life back to normal and can turn back the damaging effects caused by addiction on your life, values, and family.

STEP 3: CONSULT A PROFESSIONAL ABOUT HOW AND WHERE TO START FROM

The most important step after you have decided to overcome your addiction is to take professional help. Ask where and how to start. Some people can be treated by medicines and some are treated using other techniques like detox treatment, psychotherapy, taper technique etc.

STEP 4: TECHNIQUES TO OVERCOME OPIATE ADDICTION FOREVER

- *Detox Treatment Help*

This is the first step to treating opiate addiction. This is the removal of drugs from the system of an addict.

For most people, withdrawal effects of opiates keep them from taking the very first steps towards living a drug-free life. Detox programs offer psychological as well as the physical support that a person requires in order to stop utilizing drugs.

During this treatment, addicted people stop taking opiates and they allow their bodies to adjust to living without drugs. During this time period, ***withdrawal symptoms*** are experienced by people including:

- Cold sweats
- Diarrhea
- Depression
- Irritability
- Muscle aches and pains
- Vomiting
- Tremor
- Cramps
- Perspiration
- Flu-like symptoms
- Suicidal ideations
- Panic attacks

These symptoms continue for about 7 to 10 days in most of the cases. Though these symptoms are uncomfortable, they do not pose any substantial threat to the recovering addict. Opiate withdrawal is an important step in detoxification process but when individuals detox in a treatment or medical setting, many withdrawal symptoms can be subverted or at the least controlled by the use of rest, medication and many other methods of care and treatment.

Over-the-Counter Cures

Getting through pains, chills, fever, and aches is what overcoming opiate addiction is about. Ibuprofen, Tylenol and some of the other "non-addictive" pain alleviating agents could help in easing some of your discomforts.

Taper Technique

This technique slowly and gradually reduces the amounts of dosage over time. This approach is helpful in reducing the withdrawal effects as the body would only have to adapt to minor reductions. Only can this be helpful if you stick to the plan and do not cheat i.e. do not get back to using drugs again.

Buprenorphine

Buprenorphine is used to treat opiate addictions as one of the therapies of opiate-replacement. This medication mimics the outcomes of opiates, but it does not pose a higher addiction risk. Buprenorphine could also be given by physicians as they have the authority to prescribe it.

Changes in Daily Routine

Most often the addiction of opiate spawns a lifestyle of its own. Habits or routines, like utilizing opiates before going to bed (i.e. sleep) or using them before going to work will have to be replaced with some healthy alternatives. Making a plan ahead of time could help.

Attending Support Groups

Support groups provide a source of support, guidance and camaraderie when trying to overcome opiate addiction. The group members in the support group share their experiences and extend their advice on the process of recovery and also cope during the hard times. There is no one to criticize which makes people comfortable. Support groups also help overcoming the depression that is caused as a result of sitting alone.

Psychotherapy

Psychological addiction should be equally treated like the physical addiction. Psychotherapy treatment helps addicts recover through the forces that drive them to use opiates. This is also known as a behavioral treatment which involves an intensive therapy through talk. Through this procedure, people build up positive self-concepts.

Residential Treatment Programs

For people who have been relying on opiates since a long time require intense drug treatments. Comprehensive and structured care is provided by residential treatment programs and they are designed for helping the users to abstain from opiates for a long-term period until the person will no longer crave the drug.

"Residential opiate addiction treatment centers" provide an extensive range of specialized services and treatments that are designed especially to help people in overcoming their opiate addiction and helping them live a life free of drugs. These centers provide people the required group supports, ongoing psychotherapies, and medical care as effective methods for their opiate addiction treatment. Also, these centers closely supervise the people and give them ongoing care so they can resist the cravings (these come with the withdrawal).

Those who are in the recovery process have a higher potential of an overdose for them preventing relapse is very important to avoid the likelihood of an overdose. These centers use intensive treatment approaches which reduce the chances of a relapse.

"Residential opiate addiction treatment centers" offer the recovering addicts with a complete 24-hour access to therapists and counselors, who are specialized in dealing with issues of opiate addiction.

Outpatient Treatment Programs

People who have completed their residential program could gain from ongoing treatments that are offered through outpatient programs. Though these programs are less restrictive, they help the addicts in staying engaged during the recovery process and develop skills required to cope with everyday life.

Outpatient programs offer support and help to people while allowing them to stay at home. This treatment does not require residential care or hospitalization. The decision of choosing outpatient treatment depends entirely on the severity of the problem.

Different stages of "outpatient treatment" used to treat opiate addiction include counseling, detoxification, long-term support, and aftercare. People with severe opiate addictions should not opt for outpatient treatments.

INDIVIDUAL TREATMENT NEEDS

It is important that a person receives the right treatment or else no efforts will help them in overcoming opiate addiction. This case is particularly for long-term users of opiate. The first and most important step is to understand what kind of treatment will help you.

Each of the above-mentioned methods of treatment provides individuals with some medical support or monitoring, therapy and counseling, detox and aftercare. Some of these programs are longer as compared to the others. In order to make the opiate addiction treatments effective and safe, researchers propose that the programs should be of 90 days at least, and in severe cases they can be longer too. Research has shown that it takes about 90 days in order to effectively break the habit and to bring changes in the behavior. For some people, it might take longer to overcome their addiction of opiate.

MEDICATIONS THAT CAN TREAT OPIATE ADDICTION

If you opt for treating your addiction then the following medications can help. But always consult a professional before using these.

- Revia (naltrexone)
- Suboxone, Subutex (buprenorphine)
- Methadone

Overcoming opiate addiction requires willpower. Counseling and medication can improve chances of success. With the invention of new drugs like naltrexone and buprenorphine (sometimes they are combined with naloxone) and therapies like methadone and also the 12-step programs, have been successful in helping thousands of people to recover from opiate addiction.

*Naloxone and Buprenorphine are combined rather than using intravenous (IV) lines.

One of the standard treatments for treating opiate addiction requires methadone. This is an oral long-acting opioid which helps in keeping withdrawal, relapse and cravings under control. Methadone is helpful for opiate addicts as it rehabilitates them and prevents the symptoms of withdrawal which can motivate to continue using drugs. Naltrexone and naloxone are medications which oppose opioid receptors; this means that they can curtail the opiate urge by blocking the receptors of opiate so that when opiates are taken, they are unable to produce gratifying effects. The blockers alone sometimes are helpful for addicts who are highly propelled to quit. Also, scientists are preparing a durable version of naltrexone which would be required to be taken only once in a month.

Suboxone is another medication that can be used for detoxing and withdrawing from opiates. This medicine is a combination of buprenorphine (which is a mild opiate) and naloxone. Naloxone is a medication which reverses opiate's effects if it is taken intravenously.

Suboxone should supposedly to be taken as a tablet and it should be kept under the tongue. But in cases when Suboxone is dissolved and is taken in an intravenous manner, the naloxone turns back the buprenorphine effects, which then blocks the "high" feeling. Thus, there is less risk of diversion.

Buprenorphine medicine has a comparatively weak effect onto the receptors than methadone and it creates a limited "high", which discourages an addicted person from misusing the medication itself. Buprenorphine has been given to many patients and it has proven to be helpful. It is used in treating heroin addiction.

Dangers, Effects and Side Effects of Suboxone

- It is potentially addictive.
- Withdrawal symptoms are likely to be experienced as you break off Suboxone.
- If soon after another opiate Suboxone is taken, you might experience symptoms of withdrawal.
- Suboxone could increase the sleepiness due to alcohol or other drugs.
- An overdose of Suboxone is likely to result in seizures, slow breathing, loss of consciousness, confusion, coma and death.

Suboxone Withdrawal

Suboxone, like other opiates do if stopped too quickly, causes symptoms of withdrawal such as irritability, low energy, sweats (hot and cold), anxiety, muscle pains and aches, nausea, abdominal cramping, diarrhea. Many people feel that withdrawal from Suboxone is difficult just like the withdrawal from methadone.

STEP 5: COPING WITH THE WITHDRAWAL SYMPTOMS

If you are an opiate addict and want to get rid of it, then the only way is to stop taking these drugs. When you stop taking drugs, you will have to face withdrawal symptoms, as your body is used to them. Many addicts keep taking opiates to avoid these symptoms. The process of withdrawal is inevitable. Nothing is impossible; all you require is willpower and determination.

HOME REMEDIES FOR COPING WITH WITHDRAWAL SYMPTOMS

People who are dependent on opiates, their bodies get used to them. The bodies develop tolerance to many different side effects of drugs, such as constipation and dryness. A strong reaction might be caused when these people stop taking opiates.

If you ever think about or are already thinking about going through withdrawal all by yourself, you will have to prepare yourself. Try tapering off opiates slowly before you stop using them completely, this will limit the withdrawal intensity. Nonetheless, due to the addiction's compulsive nature, almost all the people find it difficult to gradually reduce a number of opiates they take thus, they return back to their addiction.

Dehydration due to diarrhea and vomiting (withdrawal symptoms) is common which could result in serious health complications. Most of the people, due to dehydration, end up being in the hospital. During withdrawal, it is important to drink enough of hydrating fluids. Electrolyte solutions, like Pedialyte, might help in keeping you hydrated.

Over-the-Counter Help

Usage of right doses of over-the-counter medications could help. For diarrhea, take loperamide (Imodium). If you feel nauseated, try taking medications like dimenhydrinate (Dramamine) or meclizine (Bonine or Antivert). You can also take antihistamines like Benadryl. Pains and aches that appear unexpectedly and suddenly anywhere could be treated with NSAIDS like ibuprofen (Motrin, Advil) or acetaminophen (Tylenol).

Withdrawal symptoms could last for a few days or a few weeks. When taking medications for withdrawal symptoms, be very careful and stick to the recommended dose. If you think the regular dose is not making you feel better, then discuss the problem with your doctor.

Stay Safe and Comfortable

When going through withdrawal try staying comfortable. Keep yourself busy with books, movies or any other distraction. Make sure to have extra sheets, soft blankets, and a fan. Due to excess sweating you might have to change your bedding.

Make sure to tell about your withdrawal attempt to your family members or friends. You always need someone to keep a check on you. Be very vigilant of anecdotal stories and recipes described on different online forums. They have not been rigorously tested for efficacy and safety.

It is extremely important to keep yourself and your mind engaged and occupied. Do things that you enjoy in order to increase endorphins of your body. This can ameliorate the chances of long-term success.

TREATING WITHDRAWAL

Some of the treatment methods could decrease the severity and length of the symptoms in order to make the opiate withdrawal process easy. Your doctor might suggest the following medications:

- clonidine hydrochloride for treating common symptoms
- naloxone for reducing the occurrence of symptoms
- naltrexone for treating and reversing a heroin overdose
- anesthesia for a speedy detoxification

Doctors also prescribe buprenorphine to keep people from relapsing after detox. Sometimes during the treatment, Buprenorphine is combined with naloxone. In cases of severe methadone addiction, physicians might ask you to take the drug and then step by step decrease the dosage over time in order to reduce the dependence naturally.

STEP 6: WHAT TO DO IF YOU RELAPSE

During the recovery process, there is always a risk for relapse. Relapse is very common among the addicts and it should be expected. As the withdrawal process is painful, individuals at some point quit and get back to taking opiates. Relapse is one of the stages of opiate addiction treatment.

Some people begin their recovery process from where they left off after relapsing.

Opiate addictions leave long-lasting impressions on the chemical functions and processes of the brain. These effects then make the recovering addict capable of relapsing for the years to come.

Relapse causes vary from person to person:

- Daily life pressures
- Co-occurring conditions, like anxiety disorders and depression
- Lack of social support
- Interpersonal conflicts
- Poor coping skills
- Lack of dedication in recovery process

Starting again with the opiate addiction treatment after you have relapsed could help you in identifying your problem areas and taking different steps in order to strengthen your recovery process.

After a relapse treat yourself by psychotherapy. It will take a few weeks and will ensure that you do not relapse again.

CONCLUSION

Nothing in life is impossible; all you need is determination and support to achieve your goals. An addiction can disturb and destroy the life of an individual completely. Take professional help before it's too late.

Many people run away from recovery process due to the fear of withdrawal. Opiate withdrawal could be painful. Most of the addicts quit before the withdrawal process starts. Abusing opiates shortly after you have attempted to quit could increase the risk of death. Withdrawal is difficult, but not life threatening. If you have been successful in overcoming the withdrawal symptoms, then the next step is to make a plan for a long-term success. This includes mental health treatments as well as support groups.

Many people, who go through opiate addiction treatments, relapse after some time. This is very common and should be expected. At this stage, one of the most important things individuals can/should do is to get back on their recovery horse.

Stay positive, calm and relaxed. Nothing is easy to achieve. You will have to put in a little extra effort to get back to your normal life. Stay determined and nothing can stop you from overcoming your opiate addiction forever. Many people have been successful in overcoming their addictions and you can be one of them. Keep trying!

Hope you learned significant things from this book. Good luck on all your endeavors!

Finally, if you enjoyed this book, then I'd like to ask you for a favor, would you be kind enough to leave a review for this book on Amazon? It'd be greatly appreciated!

To Leave a Review go to :
http://www.amazon.com/dp/B010I6GMQQ

Preview of 'Alcoholism And Addiction Cure: The Ultimate Step-by-Step Guide to Alcohol Addiction Treatment'

Chapter 1: What is Alcoholism?

Definition

What is **Alcoholism**? The answer to that question usually depends on who you ask. Alcoholism means different things to different people and groups and guess what? They are all correct.

By definition, alcoholism is an addiction to the consumption of alcohol. Simply put, it is the term coined for when drinking alcohol becomes a problem. In medical terminology, alcoholism is the physical and mental condition that is present when one is addicted to alcohol. The unabashed definition is "Misuse, problem use, abuse, and heavy use refer to improper use of alcohol which may cause physical, social, or moral harm to the drinker." And if you ask someone in the Twelve Step program of Alcoholics Anonymous, you would most likely hear that alcoholism is a disease with physical, mental, emotional, and spiritual dimensions and the only way to be free from the clutches of the disease is total abstinence from alcohol.

Manifestations

The manifestations of alcoholism are quite a lot. Some are extremely obvious and others are not outwardly apparent at all. Within the confines of alcoholism, there are signs that alcohol is being abused and is becoming or already is a problem and there are manifestations that indicate there is an addiction present.

What is the difference between abuse and addiction? Abuse is the improper use of alcohol, which includes drinking for the wrong reasons, drinking for too many reasons, making bad decisions regarding drinking such as drinking while driving and other indications that the consumption of alcohol is beginning to get out of hand.

Addiction is when you are dependent upon alcohol. It is when drinking rules your life and everything done is centered on alcohol. It is the physical and mental dependence on alcohol to make it through each and every day.

Signs that indicate alcohol is being abused

Constantly thinking of having a drink. You may be at work or at school but in your mind you are planning your next drink. Thoughts of having a drink are beginning to become an obsession during this stage, whether you are acting those desires out or not, it is a problem.

- **Making poor choices centered on alcohol**. When you get behind the wheel of the car after having one or too many or actually pop open a beer while driving, it is an indication that alcohol is becoming more important to you than making good, sound decisions.

- **Blacking out**. When you go out drinking and don't remember where you parked the car and it turns out to be in the yard, that is called "blacking out". It is different than simply being drunk. It is a period of time where you have no recollection of the events that happened during your drinking spree. Anything could have happened and oftentimes, it does.

- **Hurting yourself and/or others**. Putting alcohol before the safety of yourself and others is a sign that you are abusing it. Some who drink become violent and abusive when under the influence. Knowing that someone will possibly or probably get hurt when you indulge and doing so anyway is a big red flag.

- **Legal issues**. If you have been arrested for driving under the influence or have had legal problems resulting from alcohol in any way, your partaking is very possibly escalating to the point of abuse. Writing a hot check to obtain alcohol, physically fighting with someone while under the influence and stealing a six-pack are all examples of activities that can lead to a trip to jail. If you have been arrested due to an alcohol related crime, you are in no uncertain terms abusing alcohol.

- **Medical issues**. Is drinking causing physical effects that you are ignoring because you choose to keep it up? If your liver is giving in, you are not eating right or if your resistance is being lowered due to the fact you are consuming alcohol, you are abusing it.

- **Concern of family and friends**. Once friends and family begin to note any, part or all of the things above, they become concerned. Oftentimes when they begin to voice the concerns of alcohol abuse, it pushes the abuser one way or the other. Some seek treatment or solutions for their desire to drink before it gets full-blown out of hand. Others shrink into themselves, continue to give in to the temptation and proceed down the destructive path towards alcohol addiction.

- **Indications of Alcohol Addiction**
- **Use of alcohol spirals uncontrollably**. When you cannot control your drinking habit and cannot quit, it is considered an addiction. At this point, it is an extremely serious condition that must be stopped. It is said that the path of addiction leads to one of three places: jail, institution or death. There is but one option and that is the road to recovery.
- **Obsession**. You have become completely consumed with a one track mind -- alcohol! You spend your days (and nights) acquiring, consuming and plotting to get more. No longer do any other outside activities matter, friends and family are tossed by the wayside.
- **Withdrawal**. When you do not have alcohol in your system, you feel sick. **Symptoms** may include nausea, fever and even tremors.
- **Medical Conditions**. You begin to suffer from physical ailments due to alcohol such as reddening of the nose and cheeks, gastritis, stomach issues and general poor health.
- **Tolerance**. Your tolerance level changes. You begin to require more alcohol to feel the effects or to keep withdrawals away. While a six-pack used to get you feeling tipsy, it now takes two or three.

Standard Alcohol Drinking versus Alcohol Abuse

There is a fine line separating the distinction between social drinking, alcohol abuse and alcohol addiction. When you are passing from one stage to the next, you hardly notice it until you have already crossed over. That is one thing that makes alcoholism so deceiving. In Alcohol Anonymous (AA), it is referred to as a cunning and baffling disease.

Although alcoholism is an addiction like having a heroin habit is, it's not as forthcoming. While a junkie must go to the dope house and score his fix, an alcoholic merely walks into the local liquor store and leaves with his (or hers). A meth addict certainly wouldn't do a bump in public but an alcoholic can fit right in at any bar, restaurant or company party. It's socially acceptable to drink yet not socially acceptable to be a drunk. Where is the line drawn and how exactly is the line defined?

Because standard, or social, alcohol drinking is so acceptable, many alcoholics have gotten their start by consuming it like others do but one thing led to another and their drinking got out of control. A man who liked to have a few beers with friends or a highball at business lunches may pump his alcohol consumption up a notch when his wife of twenty years walks out of the marriage with his best friend. And who wouldn't? Sometimes a situation that life dishes out is the root of alcohol abuse.

Others seem to be genetically pre-dispositioned for disaster when it comes to alcohol. While some scientists attribute it to actual genes, AA gurus say it all due to the disease of alcoholism and many religious teachings say it is the lot of a sinner. One thing's for certain, some people have a problem with alcohol from the first time it ever touches their tongue.

While some people are content with a drink or two on a social occasion, there are others who take it to the next level. They don't stop with one or two and find that "one is too many and a thousand is never enough." Not only do they overdo the amount of alcohol they consume, they drink too often as well.

We've all witness this in action. Joining in a toast of champagne at a wedding is a social gesture, often followed by a drink or two during the dance and reception. Everyone is happy and joyous and perhaps some are even a little tipsy. Then there seems to always be at least one in the crowd who cannot handle their liquor. They get rowdy, obnoxious and out of control before the night is over. When the rest of the guests have long since put down their drinks, he (or she) is just getting started. The big drinker often says or does things that are not socially acceptable and many times does not even remember doing so once he or she sobers up. For these people, social drinking is far from social and the behavior they display is certainly not acceptable.

When alcohol becomes a problem, it is exactly that -- a problem. Alcohol abuse is using alcohol like a drug. A social, or normal drinker, would not drink because his or her finances are in disarray. They would most likely find that to be a reason not to drink for it costs money. An alcohol abuser, on the other hand, will find lack of finances to be a reason to drink even more. Likewise, a normal drinker would not continue to drink if his or her spouse threatened to divorce him or her if they did so. But an alcohol abuser will drink although there are extreme reasons not to.

When a social drinker crosses over to abusing alcohol, the chances of him or her becoming an alcoholic is very great. It generally takes a bottoming out of sorts to jolt him or her back to reality and to give up drinking. When that line is crossed and the person is unwilling to quit, he or she is usually nearing the stage where they are drinking so much on a regular basis that their body becomes physically addicted.

Then, not only has the line between social drinking and alcohol abuse been crossed but the line between alcohol abuse and alcohol addiction has been crossed as well. This is when, if there is no change, there is sure to be disaster.

Oftentimes there is denial that comes along with the problems of abuse or addiction so it is common that it will take an awakening in order to stop the madness. The awakening may come in the form of a trip to jail, killing someone in a car wreck while drunk or simply reaching the pits of despair. Sometimes, it is an intervention of family and friends that gets the recovery process started. Oftentimes, the alcoholic refuses to seek help regardless of consequences, confrontation or any other condition and ends up in a jail or prison system, mental institution or dead.

According to the National Institute on Alcohol Abuse and Alcoholism, content varies with the type of Alcohol such as wine, beer, or malt liquor. Regular beers have 5% alcohol content whereas several light beers have 4.2%. In the United States, a standard drink includes 14 grams of pure alcohol seen in 5 ounces of wine with a 12% alcohol, 12 ounces of regular beer, and 1.5 ounces of distilled spirits which contains approximately 40% alcohol content.

Maybe you wonder how you will know that you already have too much. There are markers that can serve as basis for one "**Standard Drink**". A 12 fl. ounces of regular beer with 5% alcohol is one. Another instance is drinking 5 fl. ounces of 12 % alcohol content Table Wine which is equal to an 8-9 fl. ounces of malt liquor having a 7% alcohol concentration. Lastly, 1.5 fl. ounces shots of 80 poof spirits such as vodkas, whiskeys, tequilas, rums, or gins with a 40% alcohol content is still considered a Standard drink.

Chapter 2: Effects of Alcohol

What Happens to your Brain and Body when Drinking Alcohol?

While having a small glass of red wine to relax in the evening is said to be good for your heart, drinking excessively or too frequently is not. Not only does the overconsumption of alcohol cause potential problems to arise on a personal level, but it also leads a way to many physical issues as well. The effects that alcohol has on the brain and the body in just one night of partying are astounding. The effects of saturating the brain and body with it over a period of time can be grave.

Alcohol's Effect on the Brain. Alcohol is made of ethanol, a neurotoxic psychoactive drug. Sound scary? Well, it is. Although alcohol has been used in beverages for recreational, social and medicinal reasons throughout history, it is actually quite dangerous to the body.

Alcohol, or ethanol, is a depressant. It suppresses the central nervous system, which means it slows down the rate in which the brain functions. Neurotransmission levels are greatly decreased when alcohol is present in the brain. Stimulation and arousal are also depressed, meaning the activity of the brain is not working at full speed. When you are driving with alcohol in your system and see an oncoming car, your brain does not react with the speed and clarity it does when you are sober. The greater the percent of blood alcohol content you have in your system, the slower and more distorted your brain perceives things, including danger.

Check out the rest of Alcoholism And Addiction cure: The Ultimate Step-by-Step Guide to Alcohol addiction treatment on http://www.amazon.com/dp/B010I6GMQQ

65326841R00024

Made in the USA
Lexington, KY
10 July 2017